# Painting

## *Complete Guide to Watercolor Painting for Beginners*

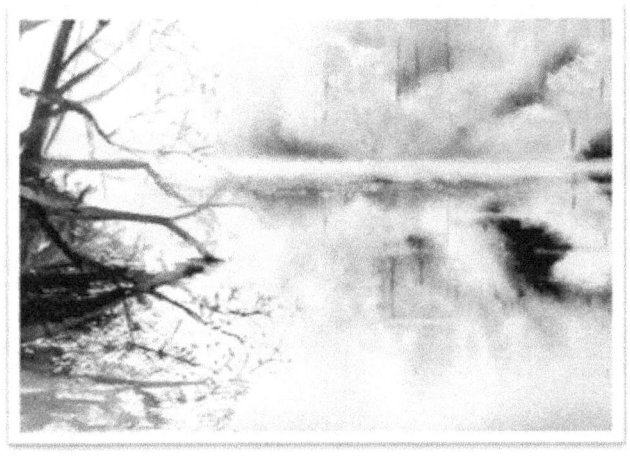

*Image: Creative Commons Attribution: Patriszkarch*

# Table of Contents

# Introduction

If you have never had the opportunity to use watercolors but think that this could be something that you would be fairly good at, then it isn't as complex as people may imagine. In fact, watercolor painting is very satisfying indeed with only the most basic of knowledge and the minimum of tools.

This medium has been used for very detailed work or dreamy landscapes that seem to go off into infinity. The variations on the types of paintings that you can produce with minimal knowledge really are incredible. For many who take up watercolors, this is a hobby that's maybe been put on the back shelf for a long time. The individual may love the finish of watercolors, but may not have had the time or confidence to try their hand at creating a watercolor image. It's time to try it out because watercolor really is satisfying. Don't be tempted to under-estimate the worth of good quality paints and paper. If you do, you will get disappointing results. The trouble with many newcomers to the craft is that they plumb for cheap paints, cheap papers and the results that they get are not actually representative of what they are capable of producing because of the lack of quality of the materials being used.

This book is devoted to those newcomers who want to try something that's traditional, but that can also be as complex as the artist wishes it to become. As skills are learned, the artist will find their own feet within the art, although at the beginning, it's vital to take pointers from those more experienced, so that the tools chosen are the right ones and the student is shown how to use them. This book is for those very people who have no experience, but would like to incorporate watercolor painting into their spare time. Be prepared to learn all about perspective, about shading and about the use of the color wheel. It's all interesting stuff and can make your artistic experience something where you are learning new techniques all of the time. Watercolor is extremely forgiving and although there are those who say you can't correct mistakes, you really can if you get them quickly enough.

Many who do choose this pastime find that watercolors are very adaptable to a particular style and thus develop their own style as they go. Each individual picture is different and the amount of water added to the image, the way the background is built up and the composition all add to the individual style of the artist.

With the use of this book, you will find your journey into the world of watercolor takes an easy leisurely route, allowing you to try out color mixing and washing and experiment with different brush techniques, which add texture and depth to the work that you produce. Remember to experiment yourself as well with colors, wet on dry, dry on wet and with different brushes so that you make the most of the experience. You will find a method that you prefer as most watercolor painters do tend to find a specialty and stick to it.

There are artists who are particularly good at portrait work, while others prefer to draw wild and barren scenery or use the delicacy of water color to produce pictures of flowers and natural scenes. Water colors are not just delicate do don't make the mistake of thinking that you cannot achieve bold color when using it. You really can. Some artists that prefer to use watercolor produce stunning results by mixing thicker mixes where less water is included but like the use of watercolor because it allows such fine detail to be painted onto the paper as well as having a wonderful range of colors and paintbrushes tailored to its use.

If you Google the idea of watercolor flowers, for example, you will see how vast the scale is of how light and delicate or how stunningly beautiful and strong colored different artists are. Watercolor is such a fine medium that it is favored by artists worldwide for being able to give their pictures such depth and such delicacy all at the same time. Yes, your work will be flat, but the detail won't be and for those who prefer a thinner medium and more control over their work, watercolor is ideal.

When I started painting, I used acrylics because I wanted strong colors. However, what I didn't realize was that if you buy great quality paints, you can achieve the same with watercolor and make your painting so much more delicate and detailed. In fact, I haven't looked back since, which is why I am so intent on sharing this medium with readers. Oil paints? Not really my scene at all. They are difficult to work and the pigments scare me a little but with water based paints, you don't have that same stigma and you can really try out so many different techniques. When you see the wide range of different styles all using watercolor, that's got to tell you that there has to be a style that suits you. Whether your style is dreamy and gives the impression of floating, or whether its detail orientated, water color really has it all.

# CHAPTER ONE

# Tools Needed

When beginning my late career as a watercolor artist, I made the mistake of thinking that I needed all of the brushes displayed in the watercolor section of the craft shop. There was a tempting array of brushes available, though what I learned over a period of time was that in the initial stages of painting, I needed very few. The brushes that you will need when you start watercolor painting will include one which is sufficiently wide for backgrounds and another for detail. The brush choices that you will find in an art shop will include these, though you don't need them all at this time. The feathering brush is something that I tried and feel that I wasted money on because for watercolors, it didn't really do anything useful that I couldn't do with other cheaper brushes.

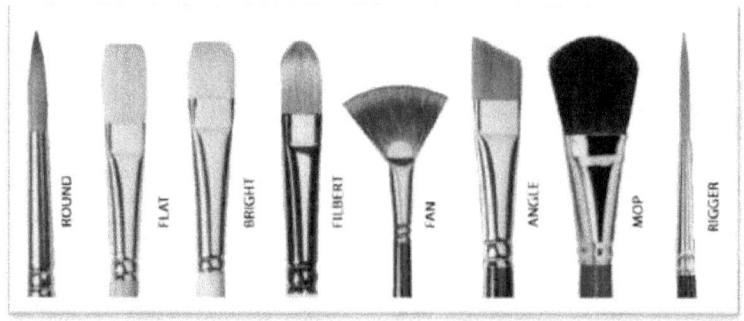

The most useful of these at the beginning of your painting experience will be the rigger which is used for detailed work and which should be of reasonable quality and the flat brush with plenty of brush length. This will be used for washes. The rigger has longer bristles and the purpose of this brush is that it holds a lot of water and can be used for lining detail. You will notice on brushes that there are sizes marked and a triple zero for example would be a brush with very little hair. These fine brushes are something that watercolor painters get rather attached to because they allow very fine detail. Round brushes are also something that water-color artists use a lot from fine all the way through the spectrum to a thickness of 16. There's something worth knowing about brushes that you may not be aware of. Different manufacturers may produce what have the same numbers, but the actual brush size can vary by manufacturer. You will get used to your favorites but never buy cheap brushes. It will be a disappointing experience. A good quality art shop will display various makes and you also have the choice of brush length. A longer brush is a good idea for the detail orientated painter because it allows them to step back from their work and take a look at it from a distance. This gives a much better impression of what people will see from the normal distance of viewing a picture. Close up you can't always see this.

The brushes that you buy need to be primed before use. That's because they have a factory finish and the bristles should be cleaned with clean water. To dry the brush sufficiently to use it, simply use a flicking action and see that the brush bristles come to a fine point at the end. You may even be able to ask the art shop to do this for you when choosing brushes because they know that artists are fussy about their choice of brushes and the signs that the brush is good quality will be that pointed tip after the bristles have been washed. If an art shop is reluctant to let you use water on a brush to see how good it is, then they are perhaps not the best art shop to use. Those that understand the relevance of the brush test are more likely to stock good quality brushes.

One kind of brush that you may find very useful is a scrub brush. This is a brush that can be used to pick up excess paint in areas where you may have laid a little too much. People say that watercolor is unforgiving but it's not as difficult as you may think. With a scrub brush, you are able to shift quantities of paint from any given area (or scrub – hence the name) and correct and imbalance of paint caused accidentally, as well as evening out paint density in a set area of the painting. I particularly like a lining brush or rigger. This is a brush which has long bristles capable of holding quite a lot of paint. If you know that you have lines to paint and you want these to be fine and consistent, then a lining brush can hold rather a lot of paint and go on drawing that line longer than you may have thought possible! Again, plumb for quality.

Other tools that will be valuable will be a pencil, pencil sharpener and eraser. The pencil should be HB since this will be a relatively hard pencil that will easily rub out and will be used to sketch shapes on your paper to give you the right dimensions of perhaps scenery or the outline of still life objects. This acts as a guide and helps you to create accurate work. It's also light enough not to leave dark traces on your paper as B pencils would.

Tracing paper is extremely helpful as you can form a grid to help you to get your image into the correct dimensions for the page. Ancillary items that may be useful to you are items such as painter's tape, an iPad if you have one (for scenery pictures and to help you to get perspective right) and, of course, paper.

The paper that you choose should always be that which is recommended for watercolors. Be aware that there are different weights of paper available. At the beginning of your experience, opting for a good quality paper of 300 gsm is a good bet. You will be able to experiment with other papers later, though this is a good weight and density for your first water color painting experiences. You will also find that papers have different finishes and it may be an idea to try different paper to see which suits your purpose. I tent to use a lightly stippled paper for portrait work because I feel it adds texture to the image, but that's personal preference. Strathmore and

Saunders produce good quality papers and are perhaps the best in the world. Since you are not spending a fortune, go for the best if you want to get the best experience.

If you have the cash, do buy yourself a pad as well because you will find that sketching while you are out and away from home will be something that you will want to do. Thus a size that is easily portable is suggested. Strathmore also make pads and these are not that expensive at all. Websites such as Amazon.com have a great range and you need to be wary of buying makes that you haven't heard of that offer you cheaper alternatives because although these may suit kids that are painting for fun, the serious artist needs serious paper!

For the time being, you don't need all the fancy trimmings such as easel and palette. You can get away with using paper plates as palettes until such time as you know if it's worth spending more money on your tools. Some people do enjoy watercolor painting very much while others move on to different hobbies, so saving on the initial outlay is wise. If you think that working in fine detail is 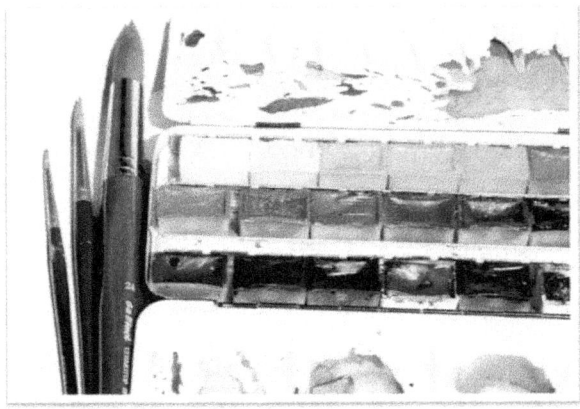 something that you may enjoy, then investment in a freestanding magnifier may also be worthwhile. Some miniature water-color painters use these because they help to see the exact placement of the brush on the paper and with find detail – that's important.

A good quality set of watercolors that includes around 12 colors should be sufficient at the beginning of your experience. If you think you will take up water color painting you can invest in a pack where the separate colors can be bought individually, thus keeping your paint set up to date and also being able to add more colors at a later stage when you get more ambitious.

Bear in mind that a lot of the work that you do with your paints will have varying color anyway depending upon the dilution of the paint, so that a plain color can indeed produce many different shades within that color range. You will also learn to mix colors on your palette, so that even 12 colors will easily be sufficient for your painting needs.

These can be in tube format or in block format as this makes little difference to the use of the paints. Established artists often prefer block. One thing that you should be aware of is that quality is important. It's better to have a good quality artist's set of watercolors than to buy the cheapest you can find because the results will be so much better. Since these are not overly costly, it's not a deal-breaker, but it will make a difference to your experience.

You may have noticed that we emphasized and emphasized again the importance of the materials being good quality. If you do try cheap materials, you really will be disappointed.

# CHAPTER TWO

# The Advantages and Disadvantages of Classes

I have added this section because I believe it's important that you go into classes or the possibility of classes knowing what this entails. I think that before you consider going for an art class, you need to meet the teacher and see the kind of work which is being produced. There's a very good reason for this. The disadvantage that some classes have that they work on a very narrow spectrum and your individuality is not permitted to surface. Teachers can have very set ideas and ideals about the work that you produce and I have known artists that have almost given up because of having bad teachers. Let's look at the advantages and disadvantages of classes:

## Advantages of classes

If you want to become social with other people who are taking up watercolor, then classes will enable you to do that. Those who have little confidence may find that classes are the ideal opportunity to start using watercolors and that the environment is a great one for learning the use of different tools and methods. Classes are normally geared toward:

- Learning about washes
- Learning about perspective
- Group outings to paint pictures
- Learning all the techniques involved

Get a great teacher who you can respect and classes can be a great experience. The teacher should be open to new artists and know that you have never done this kind of work before. The class chosen should be a beginner's class because otherwise you will find yourself feeling a little lost and in the company of people much more proficient than you are. When you get a class at your level, it's very enjoyable and fun and makes painting less solitary. You also have classmates that can help you when you get stuck on a particular technique or just want a little friendly criticism. Good classes will help you a lot, but you also need to be aware of the potential disadvantages of a class that doesn't offer such great reward.

## Disadvantages of classes

There are also disadvantages of classes and you need to be aware of these because classes may end up not being your style at all.

- The teacher won't accept your style
- The teacher has very set ideas and won't budge from them
- You learn rigid rules and tend this tends to stifle your creativity
- There is no flexibility
- You get the class showoff

There is nothing more humiliating than being told by an art teacher that you have made a mess of something or that your work does not follow what he/she is saying. I have come across many teachers who are mediocre artists at best. If they were really that good at art, how come they are teaching it rather than doing it? You have to understand that there are several schools of thought. Some artists are open to different styles and teach you how to use the tools to create your own style. Others strictly adhere to what they know and this is often limited by their own education and experience.

If you find that you don't like an art teacher, chances are that you won't learn as much as you will with an art teacher that is sympathetic and who is flexible, allowing each student to bring individuality into their art. I remember one class where the teacher obviously favored a member of the class and we were always having his style rammed down our throats and this particular student held up as the perfect example. It made beginners feel like idiots and looking back on the experience, none of us really liked the work that the "star" student was producing anyway.

Thus, classes with the wrong teacher can stifle you. They can push you in directions that you don't want to go in. Try to think of this in terms of art in general. Music is an art, but a student who wanted to learn folk music wouldn't gain much from a teacher who only taught jazz. Putting art under one "umbrella" isn't actually fair on the student. Unless the teacher is particularly gifted at watercolor, then the art class may be of little use to you. It's better to find one that is watercolor orientated and who is open to students trying new styles.

## How to find out about classes

Classes don't just take place in educational establishments. You can get a timetable from the local educational authority but before enrolling, try to find out as much as you can about the teacher and the kind of work produced. A casual call at the facility and talking to the teachers on enrolment evening will give you a good idea of the mentality of the teacher and the experience level that the class is aimed at.

Other classes may be a lot more interesting. Online classes are good and many are done in the form of Skype meetings, in between your art work at home. A teacher talks you through your style and helps you to correct or to change areas that are causing you problems. The benefit of these classes is that they are one on one.

You can also find websites that offer classes and you need to look at the level of the classes and see if there is a class for beginners, what the cost of that class is and what it involves. Some have very detailed coursework while others are a little mean with the material that they give to students. Find out what the course includes and the duration as well as the total cost and glean from the website the kind of artwork you think is likely to be taught. A wide range of watercolor pictures that is pleasing to you is much more likely to mean that the teaching methods cover a wide area.

It's worthwhile checking out what other students say about teachers, as well, so look for testimonials. Another great place to get classes or to get professional help is YouTube, where many videos show you how to create a watercolor and cover all aspects of water color painting. If there are classes attached to the video, you will find links to the website of those running the classes, but again, check out what the paintings are like and the variety that they offer. If it seems limited, go back to YouTube and find a video which features the kind of style you had in mind. Believe me, there are literally thousands. Pinterest also have a group for watercolor classes and some of the pictures you see of watercolors lead you to these classes. Again, choose a style of picture that you find particularly pleasing because the classes will be based upon the style that you are seeing and since watercolor is so diverse you need classes that cater for your tastes.

I took classes in the initial stages, but mine were traditional classes with a teacher in a classroom environment. It was a bad experience but taught me the basics. After that, I got in touch with an art teacher via Skype and we have been in touch ever since because this teacher loves art and is always able to give me such good advice when I am worried about a new technique or a new range of paints or brushes. Their expertise is well worth having because you will never be perfect and in the learning stages, it's a good idea to keep yourself open to new ideas.

CHAPTER THREE

# Perspective and Accuracy of Dimensions

This is an interesting part of painting of all kinds but in water color, it's exactly the same except for the possibility of using fluidity in your work. Let's start to explain perspective from the start because you may not have done any form of art education and may be wondering what it means.

## Why you need to use perspective

Without some kind of perspective, art looks flat. The perspective is what gives your pictures a three dimensional effect. Thus, if you were drawing a house, it would be very unlikely that it would be a square box as children draw houses.

Looking at the simple image above, you see that a child can grasp the idea that the roof is sloped, that the door is rectangle and that the windows are square. It's a picture drawn from a very simplistic angle and does not use perspective. Thus the image is very flat. When you add perspective, this includes all of the angles

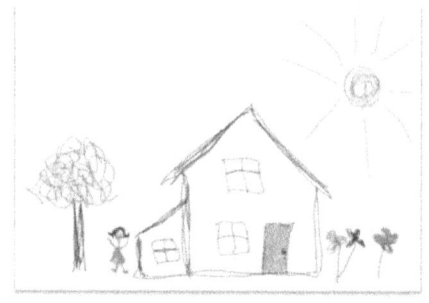

Image copyright: Shared commons: Alice Holmes

and the way that an image gets smaller as it is further away from you. Let's show you a picture that has perspective. You will instantly see the difference and that's important.

Although we know that a railway line is always going to be a standard width, it isn't when you look from one end of the line to the other. As it goes into the background, it becomes visually smaller and narrower. That's what perspective is all about. To incorporate that into your watercolor, you first need to recognize if. Look for the angle on buildings. Look where the shadows fall, as these are all things that help your picture to be drawn to perspective. I use a pencil when I am measuring for perspective and hold it up against a scene to see how large something looks. Then, when drawing

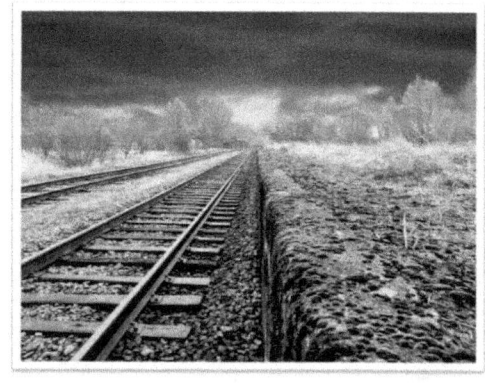

something slightly in front of that item I have drawn, I measure again and make sure that I compare the length on the pencil of the part that I am drawing.

To do this, hold the pencil horizontally and look at an object in the picture. In the case of the railway lines, I would actually hold it vertically and measure the width of the track at the furthest point, using my thumb against the pencil where the measurement is correct and then transposing that onto the paper. Then I move forward a bit with my measurement and even if you don't draw at this stage, you can make little pencil dots to give you an idea of how wide the track is at certain points all the way down your image.

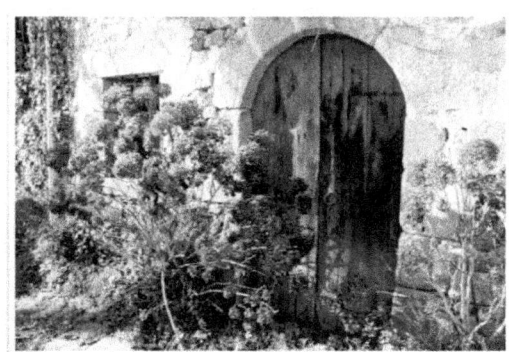

## Angles

The angles on a window sill of in a doorway are something that help them to gain perspective. If you were merely to draw a rectangle and put a doorknob on it, it wouldn't be as effective and unless that was actually what you saw would misrepresent the perspective that you were looking from. Let's show you a few examples of doorways so that you can see what I mean about using perspective.

In this picture, for example, you can clearly see the stone rebate of the door but you don't see it all the way round, because from the angle you are viewing the door, it is only visible to the top and the left hand side of the door. Look at the door itself. You can clearly see that it has a split in the center and that it opens in two, but there's more than that to it. At the central point, you have wear and tear and that needs to be noted too. Now look at the angle of the wall. Because you are looking at it from an angle, the wall that holds the door starts at the bottom right hand side of the picture and is angled toward the center at the side. That's because your perspective shows that angle.

In the case of this door, you are more or less looking straight on, so that the wall at each side of the door is actually pretty straight. However, three dimensional effect comes into the tunnel that leads to the door. Look at the width of the space between the walls and it narrows as it goes further forward because of perspective.

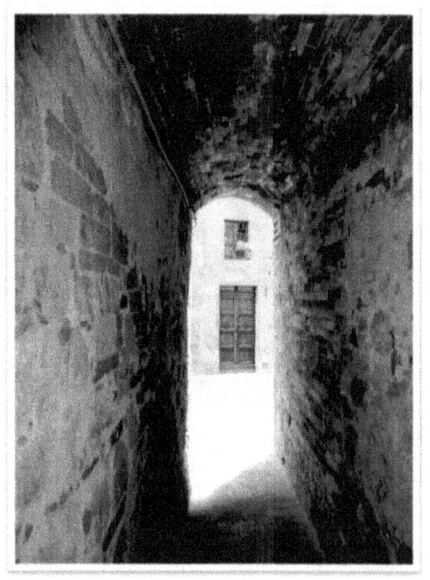

That's what you need to gage when you are sketching something. Your pencil isn't a sophisticated tool but it's a very useful one to get that perspective correct on your picture. Try practicing this because it's really important. Once you understand how to transfer perspective onto the page, you really are on your way to becoming a good artist.

CHAPTER FOUR

# The Effects of Shading

If you have ever had anything to do with drawing in any shape or form, you will have come across the relevance of shading. In the last chapter, we showed you a picture of a corridor that lead to a door. The shading in this picture was very important because it gave the picture its realistic rendition. Every object that you look at has an element of shading. Look at a pen on the table, a vase, or an object in your room and there will be darker areas and lighter areas which give the object that three dimensional rendition that people see. The armchair opposite me as I write this has dark areas where the cushions tuck into the back and the actual fabric has dark areas too where the material has been distorted by someone sitting on it. These are all important details that help your art to look more realistic. In watercolor, shading is very easy to do and there are two methods.

## Shading an orange

Let's practice shading. For this exercise, you will need the following:

- Water

- Palette or paper plate

- A medium round brush

- Watercolor paints

- Paper

Set yourself up ready to paint because we are going to show you how to use shading to the best effect. What you need to draw for this exercise is an orange, but you need to remember that not only will you have darker shaded areas but you will also have highlighted areas which are of a lighter color somewhere on the orange to make it look round.

Paint your orange directly onto the paper but beware. You are not drawing a complete circle. Leave the top area of the orange white because this is where the highlights will be placed. Thus draw a round with an area left white at the top. Did you know that blue compliments orange? On the color wheel it does and it's the perfect combination to make shadow for an orange. Mix a little blue with orange and shade the area at the bottom of the orange. Many people make the mistake of thinking that if they just add a little orange that is darker at the bottom, that's enough. You really need to learn your color wheel and learn what colors complement each other.

Look at opposing colors because this gives you an idea of what to mix for your shadows. For example orange is opposite to blue, so mixing blue and orange will give good shadow. This color wheel is worthwhile keeping because you will use it over and over again. It's a valuable resource for finding out which colors make great shadows and which colors can be blended 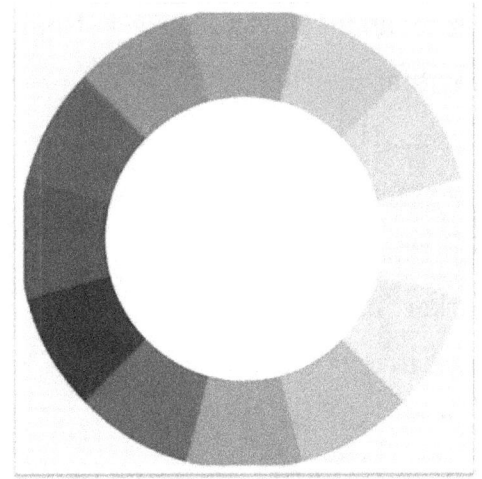 to give you shades in between the colors shown. You will get used to using it, but when you are new to watercolor painting, it's a very useful guide.

Your shadow should extend from the bottom of the orange, so that the orange begins to take on a rounded look that has depth. Then you need to work on the upper area of the orange, blending colors into that area, but being careful to leave a little of the white showing through. The thing that people forget with watercolors is that the actual white comes from the paper and is often left bare. The colors that you use at the top of the orange will be watered down a little more and lighter – almost transparent and you need to remember that an orange has a center so do leave a little of the orange white so that the center appears to look three dimensional.

Here's a picture of an orange and an apple and you can see what I mean about shadow at the bottom underneath the orange and the way that the color changes with the light as you get higher up the orange. There are also indentations in the top of the orange toward the green stem and you can add these by blending in a darker orange. You may want to try the apple as this also has similar format but instead of using blue to complement the orange, in this case, you would use a tiny bit of red as this is the color shown on the opposite side of the color wheel.

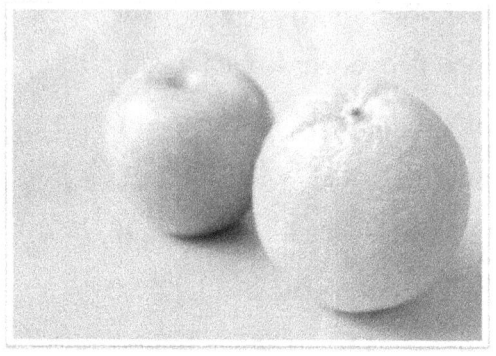

Once you get accustomed to shading using the colors on the color wheel, it takes a little bit of the mystery out of water color painting.

## Shading on faces

If you were to draw a face with no shading, again it would look very infantile. Children draw like this because they don't understand perspective. When you are painting faces, it is the shadowing that gives the face the shapes of the nose, the cheeks, the chin and all of the facial features. Look into a mirror for this exercise and using a pencil, draw the shape of your face as a flat object. Add your hair shape. Add the position for the eyes, nose and mouth. It doesn't matter how accurate the picture is. The purpose of the exercise is to show you how to use shading.

Now mix yellow and red to form a skin tone and paint the whole area of the face. We are not after accuracy. We are trying to show you blending methods that help you to create shade. Using the opposite color on the color wheel, make a shadow color with a little bit of blue and take another look into the mirror. While the original paint is still wet, use a finer brush and try to brush in the detail using the darker paint and blending it into the original color, gradually feathering it so that it runs in smoothly. The areas you note as being shadow are helping your observation skills.

This chapter is written to help you get practice. Be prepared to get out your paper and paints because that's what it's all about. The shading exercises that are being used here are things which will come naturally eventually, but for the time being you have preconceived ideas about the shapes of things. You may think in terms of a face being square, oval, long or even round. What you are not used to is looking to see the shadow that's cast on something and that's where the artist's eye is needed. Don't just see the shape. See the shadow in everything you look at and you are likely to draw or paint it in a more accurate way.

In the above example of a face, the shadow is important. You may find that you are working from photographs a lot and the amount of shadow you use really depends upon the image that you want to produce. If you were painting from the above image, a lot of the facial features are lost giving the picture a very atmospheric

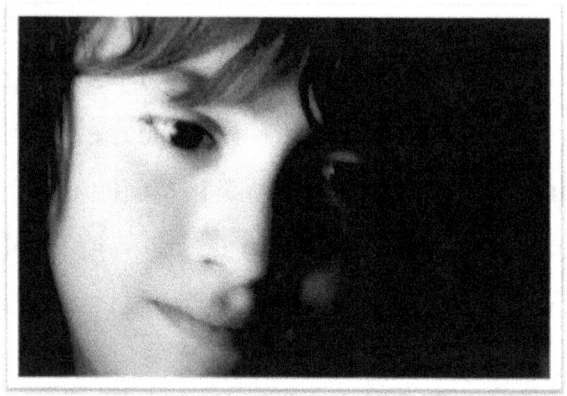

look. Note also that the skin tones are pale and that you would need to carefully mix colors to achieve the palest of the colors as the base and then add on the freckles, perhaps with a stippling brush and the shadows to the area around the mouth, the nose, cheek and eyes. Note that although you can't see the right hand side of the face, there are still some features there. This is a great image to practice with because of the contrasts and when you have finished drawing your own face, try this one just for the experience of drawing shadow. It's very difficult at first, but it becomes second nature after a while.

Look carefully at the eyes in the image because that sparkle of white is necessary. People are tempted to draw a round for an eyeball and forget that you need to let the white of the paper come through in places to give the eye that fluid look. The other problem that people have with putting an image onto their watercolor is a preconception about where everything on a face is placed when the angle that you are drawing from makes a lot of difference to the actual image. You need to forget about the way you see features and begin to actually see what's in front of you. For example, in the above photograph, the eyebrows are not straight or level because the child has her head angled. One eye is further down than the other. The lips are slanted and the nose feature isn't straight. You need to practice drawing what you see rather than using the brain's preprogrammed idea that the facial features are straight.

## Shading on buildings

We have already talked about perspective but what about the shading on a building? This part of the shading chapter covers buildings because these are a primary subject that people paint so often and they often get the shading wrong because they are not actually looking at what is there in front of them. The problem with shading on a building is that you are in the outdoors and as the sun rises and falls, the shading will change. For this exercise, I am going to show you a picture and ask you to draw it leaving out all the shading and simply taking in the shape of the building in your sketch.

It's a fairly interesting building and has lots of shapes which will help you with perspective. For the time being draw what you see without the shading because I want to show you how to make shading effective on 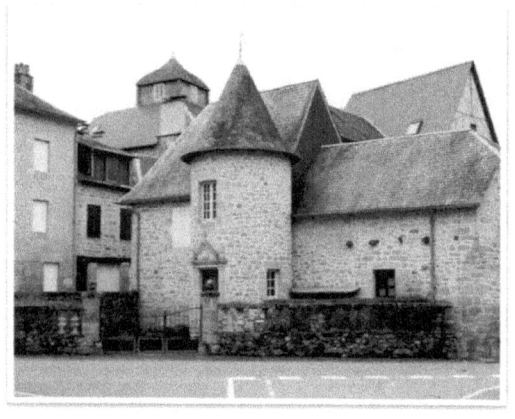 buildings. Your sketch for the time being should be in pencil and be of the rough outlines of the buildings including the tower, the roof shapes and the angles that appear in the image.

Color in your roof area because we are going to do a little detailing in this area first. The main color will of course be a murky grey. The detailing uses a very fine brush but don't worry, you don't have to get every single tile drawn, just draw in some of them to give a representation of the image that you see. Now look closely at the roof. There are areas of gray that are darker and these are your shadow areas. Load the brush with darker gray which is achieved by adding black to white. You will see that as well as the shaded areas, you have areas where lichen is seen and here you need to add a darker green to the color palette so that you can have little areas that represent the lichen.

While you have such dark colors on the palette, move down and fill in doorways that are black or window areas remembering that the white for the window frames comes from the original paper color. Add detail to the windows and doors with a very fine brush and black or gray. The walls look very complex but there's a good way to cover detail such as this. Ask yourself what the main color is. It's a very light gray beige and you need to mix quite a lot of this as there's a lot of area to cover. However, you also need to note that the color between the stones is lighter so would be used for the first wash. Then the detail of the stones is added when the first wash is dry. Because there is so much variation in color, what I tend to do is mix a whole range on the palette and dip into whatever depth of color I need for the stone that I am drawing. You don't have to be deadly accurate. You are practicing adding color and shadow and this picture was chosen for that specific purpose, because there is a lot of detail.

Now add the shadow. You will see that areas of the roof are darker than other areas and that down the side of the tower there is a line of black which gives the tower more depth. Fill in the shadow on the image and it starts to come to life. When you are working with an image that is this complex, the shadow comes last and is part of the detailing because you need to work on all of the details that make up the picture and then work toward making it look like it is in three dimensional scale.

All of these exercises take on a flexible approach. For example, if you don't like the image shown above, choose one from a magazine or one that you find online that you want to draw.

Perhaps your interest lies with boats, country scenes or something else. If so, use that idea and go with what you feel comfortable with.

# CHAPTER FIVE

# Composition of a Painting

Deciding upon the composition of your painting is important at the start. For example, if painting scenery, how much of that scenery will the picture include? The painting needs to be fairly well balanced so that those viewing it get a good overall feeling of the ambiance of the location, as well as having items within the picture nicely placed. If you look at this unfinished image by William Berryman, the reason it is used for this demonstration is because the composition is clear. The central characters were placed a little to the left and this gave room for the artist to detail the Jamaican background perfectly.

Although a little dated in style, what the picture demonstrates is composition and how this is sketched onto the paper with a pencil, which allows the artist to get an overall feel for the composition being presented. The central figures balance against the background and those seated, and no doubt had the color been added to the foliage, the overall picture would have been a pleasant combination of detail and color.

From this you can glean that you need to draw rough outlines of all items which will figure in your picture, so that you can see how well balanced the picture will be. At this stage, you can use the eraser and erase those areas that you feel need to be moved to give the picture better balance.

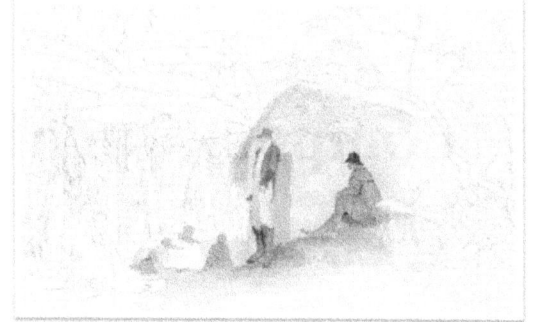

Image: Public Domain

This particular artist chooses to start coloring in the center of the image and build upon that background, since many of the leaves would actually be nearer to the eye than items such as the central point. It's a common sense approach when you have an image that uses different layers.

The composition can also be worked out on an iPad. In a recent competition for the Young Artist of the Year, a couple of the artists used an iPad to establish the best composition from different angles. What can be done with this image is that it can be transferred onto the paper using the tracing paper to create a grid. When you draw a composition using a grid, you simply sketch in the detail from each of the squares that make up that grid. Thus holding the tracing paper over the iPad screen allows you to do the same thing. One of the models for the Artist of the Year contest was amazed that the artists hardly looked at the model that they were painting. In fact, the iPad was used because it brought the detail closer to the artist and she was able to make a much better job of her painting because she had captured the detail and there was no movement of the subject.

There is also exceedingly good software available for the iPad whereby you can see the image and form a grid on the actual screen in you want to use this method and simply transpose that grid onto your paper so that everything is placed in the right position and in the right proportion.

The way to tell if your composition will work is to look at it from a distance. It should be well balanced, should have a reasonable background and foreground and the objects on that sketched composition should be pleasing to the eye. Some people use a cut out of cardboard to capture a scenery image and move this around to find out where the best picture could be created. Cardboard costs very little and is a very useful thing to have with you when on location. Look at the composition below to get an idea of how you sketch onto your paper so that your image is balanced well.

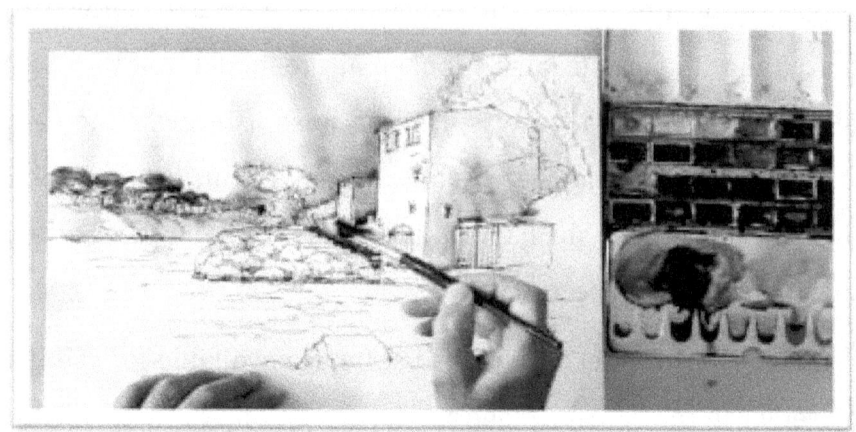

*Image: Creative Commons Attribution: Eckard Funck*

This is a well-balanced image that uses the rule of thirds. Although there is a central area of interest, your eye is drawn toward the building which is off center. That's how the rule of thirds works and it's a great way to show off your work to have good composition. You can also choose to centralize your image, or if you find that you are good at detail, use Tracy Hall's system of zooming in to get all of those great markings. Believe it or not this is watercolor and there are those that always associate water color with soft pastels, while this clearly shows attention to detail in a very artistic manner.

This is one particularly good water color artist that uses brushes that are extremely fine to create all of that almost photographic

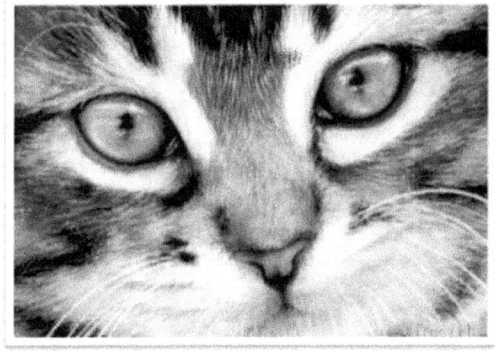

imagery. When interviewing her about her artwork, I was impressed that the amount of detail and the variety of poses that she used in her images was so varied. From miniature painting through to larger scale painting, the overall composition is always well thought out and captured. Even in busy paintings that have a lot of detail, there's a lot of thought about what goes where and this attention to detail is something that you should aim at. Using your cardboard cut-out or even using your iPad to take photographs at different angles, you can really see how best to present your work.

Tracy is passionate about detail which is why I chose her images to demonstrate what great composition is all about. If you are detail orientated, then look how cleverly all of the

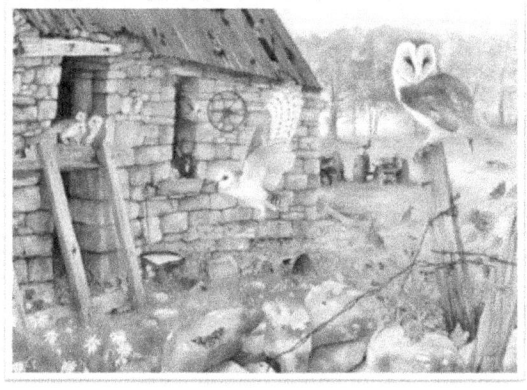

elements of this scene were captured even down to the tones of the stonework.

Think of the images that you create as a whole entity, decide what you are going to include in the image and try different angles until you are pleased with your composition.

# CHAPTER SIX

# Learning to Use Washes

**W**ashes are something that you need to experience and to play with because they determine what the background of your picture looks like or certain elements of that picture where washes are used. Washes are not just used for the background. Indeed they can be used to color a petal on a flower or to blend the paints in the area of skin on someone's portrait. A wash is merely a mixture of water color and paint that is put onto the paper and spread in a certain area to produce a specific result.

## Wet on Wet Washes

These are used where you want to produce a variety of colors washed into each other. Before you try this on a painting, why not do some examples so that you can learn how they can be performed and then choose which you need to use for your future painting. For wet on wet the idea is to apply paint to your paper with your main color after the paper has been wet. Then vary the color a little using your pallet and add this while the first color is still wet. To see how this is useful, try using contrasting colors, but don't forget to clean your brush between changing colors. Dab the wash onto the paper using a fairly large round brush and you will see that the color mixes in a very pleasant way. You will know if you have applied too much paint and this practice will help you to get accustomed to the skill. Having the wet background makes a lot of difference to the results.

## What this method can be used for

This kind of wash is useful when you are trying to produce the delicacy of the colors of petals or the complexity of the colors of the skies, for painting water or for blending colors for stonework. It helps you to have subtle differences or startling differences depending upon the colors used and it's a good idea to practice both stunning mixes and those which are more subtle and which are most likely to be used in day to day painting.

## Wet on Dry Washes

This is where you place your new color onto dry paper. It's actually the most likely plan of attack for a new artist because that's what they will have seen and it's a popular way to use water colors. One watercolor is added to dry paper and another is added and you will see that where the colors meet, there is an overlap and that different shades can be produced.

## The Advantages of Wet on Wet

This is a very useful way of creating a wash because you can get colors to flow into one another and that produces some pretty neat effects. It is kind of an evolving way to add interest to your image.

## The Advantages of Wet on Dry

It gives consistent and controllable results and what you see is what you get when it dries. That makes it much more predictable.

## Using Dry Brush Washes

Often when you are painting, you want to add color to the picture but you don't want that color to be solid. In the case of this type of wash, you do get a lot more detail. If you fill your brush with the color that you want to use, dab out the excess onto kitchen paper. I actually use this a lot and find that the reason I like it so much is that if gives you the possibility to add detail before actually using the detail brush. For areas such as the bark of a tree or the grasses in the distance or even the fields that form part of your image, this system works well. Using a flat or a large round brush, simply run the brush across the paper and think of this a bit like cross hatching in drawing. Now take the brush in the opposite direction, thus creating cross hatching with an almost dry brush.

## What Dry Brush Washes can be used for

As I said above, you can use it for any area where you don't really want solid color but you want to produce a scratch coat. The image below is a good example of where this may be used and if you think of it in terms of a scratch coat, it forms the base that is then refined by use of detail brushes.

You do need to experiment with dry brush methods because different brushes will give different effects. I have one particular brush made of hog's hair and this is a favorite for detail of this kind because of its stiffness. However this kind of shading can be used with all kinds of brushes. Make yourself a sampler using different brushes and make sure that you make a note of which brush was used because this is useful. To

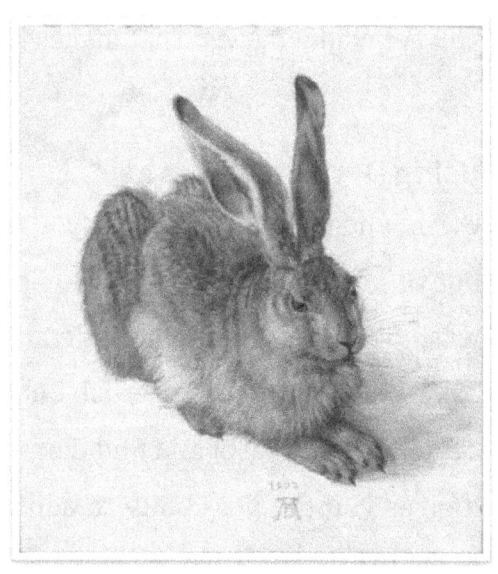

Image copyright: Albrecht Dürer - Hare, 1502 (Public Domain)

make water shine in the sunshine, this method is also very useful.

## Using dry paint on a wet surface

This is also very popular with artists because you can come up with some pretty startling results. The background wash uses color and water and then the dry paint is applied to create shapes and swirls or whatever it is that you need to draw and the detail is pretty good, but it has a certain subtlety about it that is pleasing to the eye. This could be used for the outside of buildings or for the lines which create hills in the background. It can also be used to create tree branches, but be very aware that if you want sharpness, you need to wait for the lower wash to dry a little and that if you apply the dry wash too soon, you will get blurred edges.

Washes are used in all manner of ways but these are the mainstay ways that a water color painter could use them. Practice each with different brushes. Practice with different mixes of color and you will get accustomed to what process is the best to use for the picture that you are trying to produce. It's a question of learning rather than trial and error.

For skies you would typically use a two color graded wash which allows the sky color to change as it gets lower. This graded wash can also be used for water such as in the sea and it's a clever use of washes to produce subtle changes such as would be seen in the sky or looking out toward the horizon.

Remember, the different washes and make samples using different brushes:

- Wet on wet
- Wet on dry
- Dry on wet
- Dry on dry

You can also use a water wash under your color if you want to produce really clear colors that make the most of the white background. Whatever style of wash you use, you will find that the effects of washing really is what holds watercolor apart from other forms of painting.

# CHAPTER SEVEN

# Painting Skies

Once you have sketched your scenery, the background of the picture will no doubt have sky. Often this detail is washed onto the paper before the finer detail is added. There are several ways of doing this that are explained here. For example, how much cloud is involved? If the sky is completely awash with color, then applying color with the larger brush, you can create a wash and add more color as you wash further down toward the skyline. If, however, your skies are going to be filled with clouds, this would not be as practical because you need the cloud areas to remain light. In this case, you can carefully blend your sky colors, though you do need to leave gaps where the white clouds will go. The detail on the clouds can be filled in after the wash has dried, unless you want the colors to blend in well together. In this case, you can blend them, and then use the final touch up to give the cloud more definition and three dimensional effect.

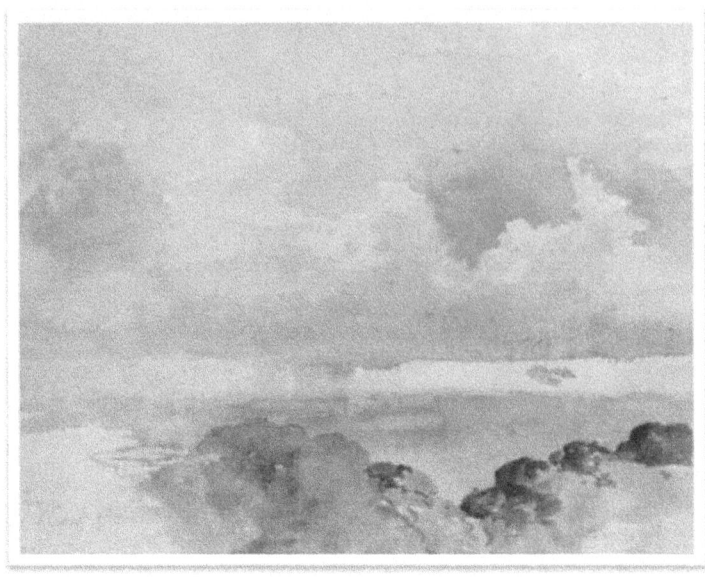

If you look on the image shown on the previous page, what this artist did was very clever indeed. He created the look of sunlight coming through the sky by limiting his shading of the sky in such a way that the sunlight appeared to be breaking through it, the colors of the sky blending in with the horizon. However, on this image, look how the overall color of the picture was set by the artist and then detail added to the cloud area, as if in a layering effect. Although these may not resemble the color of sky that you want to use, look how the cloud formations have been built up as this helps you with your work to create that three-dimensional look. If you use the lighter colors and build up from that base, you will find this is very effective indeed. Skies can look very dramatic or they can give a calming influence to the picture. However, it's a good practice to capture the sky in a photograph, particularly if the cloud formations are particularly stunning, since these are liable to disappear before you have the time to capture them.

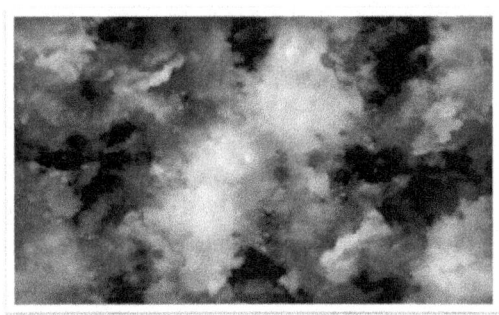

Image: Creative commons attribution: Donna Marie

Now look at the image above, as this is a very good example to give you a great range of colors that can be suitable for your sky. The artist in this case has even managed to capture that optimism which is seen when silver seems to break through a stormy sky. The movement of your brush to create this kind of detail can be a little random and light on the paper as this gives a much more detailed effect.

Maybe your first attempts at skies will not be as dramatic, although working with water colors will enthuse you to experimentation and it is this which will help you develop your skills when it comes to depicting the sky.

There are many examples of skies that you can find by simply looking at what nature is presenting you with. The color of the clouds isn't necessarily white. The blue of the sky isn't always consistent. Look further than simply seeing blue and white because all the colors in the spectrum may be included within the sky area to give it real life rendition. Clouds are not simply white areas with a little gray around them. Each sky offers its own presentation and you need to learn to capture that. In the images below, you will see how varied this can be.

Of course, nature offers much more variety than is shown here, but practicing your painting of skies will always help you to present your images in a stunning manner. Even if the sky is only a backdrop, having accurate rendition will help your picture to look great.

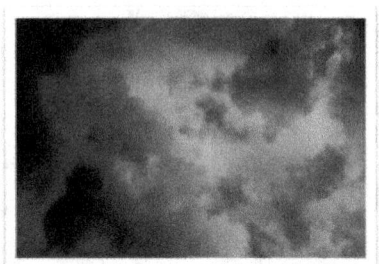

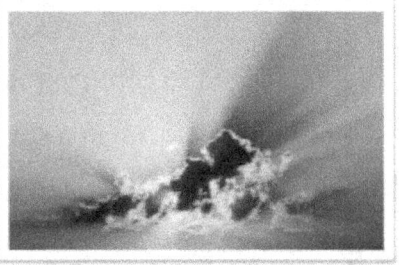

Remember as well that if you have a sky that is relatively calm, there can also be color variances which can be achieved with two or even three color graded washes as shown in the previous chapter. The way that you depict the sky really depends upon the sharpness of the image that you wish to create. Look at the yellow sky above and there is a lot of contrast that needs to be picked up. Look also at the outer areas of sky and you will see that sweeping a brush with a little color on it over the relatively somber yellow creates that look of depth.

Experiment and experiment more because the diversity of the subject matter demands it. From pastel blues right through the range to the blackest of blacks, skies are diverse and deserve to get your attention because they are the backdrop to the images that you are trying to produce with your watercolors. Don't be afraid of experimentation.

CHAPTER EIGHT

# Painting in the Horizon and Trees

The horizon and the trees, which may be in the distance, can be a bit of a task for a new painter because they are not aware of how to detail all that they see. Painting trees in watercolors doesn't have to be that complex, as the series of images in this chapter will show you. Only you can see the scene in front of you, though once you start to bring in detail to the horizon and add your trees, you really will begin to see depth appearing on your picture. Perspective is always hard for new painters but of course, the trees, which fall into the distance, will be so small in some cases that they don't actually need foliage drawn in any detail. What you see is actually a blob of color. You know it's a tree and often the mistake that artists make is trying to make that blob look too much like their own idea of what a tree should look like, rather than accepting that the blob in the distance is quite acceptable in its present format.

John Constable was an established artist who drew and painted scenery. If you look at this image, you will see that he was not too bothered about how accurate the leaves on the trees were painted. What he effectively did was use strokes of the brush to give an overall atmosphere to his work. This work gives the impression of wildness and does so very well because of the sweeping manner in which he applied the paint. The dry application is effective in this case because it gives the picture a certain amount of animation.

The detailing used on the building will have been done with fine brushes to give the shape of the buildings more substantiation. White added to the end wall of the house which forms the triangle gives it a real boost and draws the eye of the viewer toward it.

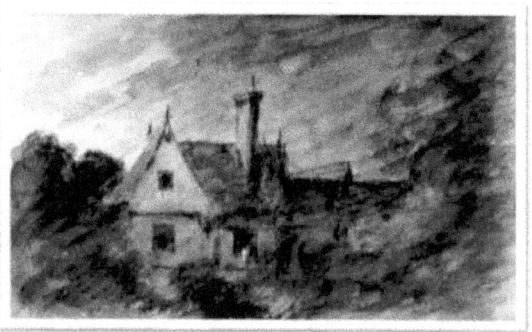

The painter shows a strong change of color where the horizon meets the sky and the wispy effect of the trees gives the painting atmosphere, while his lines and detail on the architecture give the house a strong position within the center of the picture.

In this image, what the painter was trying to do was to emphasize the cold branches and he used a very clever method to

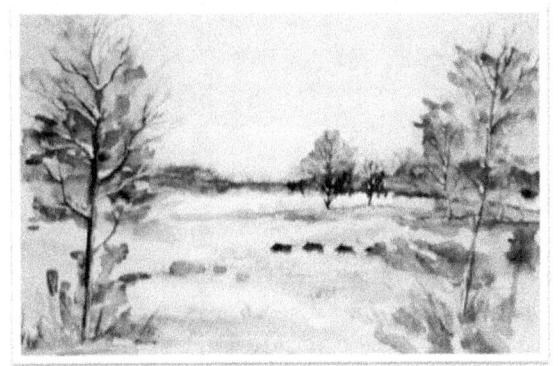

do this. The background color that was added to the trees gave him something to contrast the snow-laden branches against. The detail of branches can be added after the color and contours of trees have been painted. These would use the smaller brush and the branch detail will go up through the tree, so that the branches appear to peep out from in between the foliage.

Practice on distant bushes and hedgerows and look really closely at how the color variations work in the scene you are observing. If you try to copy nature in its rendition of color, you can't go far wrong. White or light color down the side of a branch may just give the impression of bark catching the sunlight. This also helps to give the picture a three dimensional effect.

# CHAPTER NINE

# Portrait Painting

It is just as important to compose a picture if it is a portrait as it is for any other kind of watercolor painting. Thus, your picture should aim at being balanced. Whether you decide to paint a portrait from a sideways angle or from in front, you will need to sketch the picture onto your paper with light pencil to get the perspective correct and to position where all the elements go which make up the portrait.

In the above image of Isabella by Ruben, you can see how the build-up process is performed. Look at the sketching at the bottom of the picture. This is how you begin to trace a shape onto the page. The central area shows how shading is performed and then color is introduced to the face area first with a wash, and then building up to more detail. This picture was chosen because all of the stages are shown in one image, which is perfect for an example of portraiture.

If you are working from a photograph, this is very simple. You simply need to place your tracing paper over the top of the image so you can still see the photo outline clearly. Then divide the size of the photo by drawing a grid onto the tracing paper with a line down the center, one at quarter width and then across the picture at the half and quarter width. This gives you proportion. If you look at your photograph through the tracing paper, you will see what goes into each square on your painting and be able to transpose it simply by drawing the grid onto your paper. Thus, what appears in the top left hand square is what you sketch into the top left hand square on the paper, and so on. What this does is help you to reproduce the picture from the photograph and do it to scale.

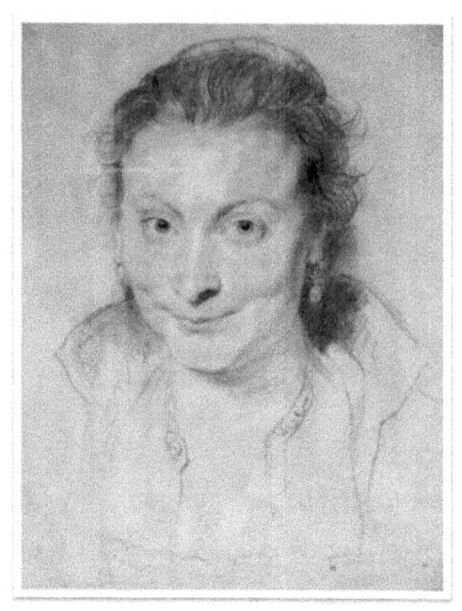

Image: Public Domain - Rubens

## Composition

The painting of a portrait gives you many choices. We have already said about the angles that you can choose, but you can also use the rule of thirds in painting portraits. There was a particular good portrait done in the Portrait Artist of the Year which really won acclaim. The portrait was done in a specific way because the artist wanted not only to show the face of the subject, but the uniform and the contrast against a window seat upon which he was kneeling looking out toward the garden. What was stunning about the image was the way in which the contrasts worked so well. Your subject doesn't have to be central, but if you are going to paint them to one side, you need to think of the background that will be used to balance off the whole effect.

Another portrait that was done for the contest was interesting because it showed the model's head balancing an apple on it and the head was slightly angled. It looked very effective indeed, but I suppose that what I am trying to say is that the choice of your composition is completely up to you. However, you do need to consider it before you start the painting because you may regret the placement of the figure as you progress if you don't think it out in advance.

## Producing skin tones

Skin tones may seem a little difficult at first but they are really easy once you know how. You will need to mix a variety of colors on your palette because the skin on a face will consist of many tones. If you look very carefully you may find hints of a mixture of reds, yellows and white. Mix these three colors together and you get a skin tone. However, mix various mixes on the palette and you also get the skin tones it takes to highlight a lighter area or shade a darker area.

When you paint a face, paint the overall skin tone as a backdrop to your shading and highlighting and then gently add tones to the painted work to give the face shape. You do need the fine paintbrush but if you find that this does not mix the different hues satisfactorily, you can use a cotton bud to help blend certain areas.

At the stage when you are painting the skin tones, the only thing you need to know other than the tones to be used is the position of the facial features. These will eventually emerge when you add highlight and shading, though for now, concentrate on getting the color tones correct.

## Noses and Mouths

The above image may help you to see how shapes are formed for the lips and nose. These are difficult areas and of course not all mouths and noses are the same, though with help of this guide, you will see how the shapes are formed and can form yours using this method. With watercolors, you need to use a small brush to set out the features and you also need to blend colors into each other to get the skin texture that you seek, as well as the shading around the nostrils and in the central area of the lips. There are some great guides on YouTube that go into

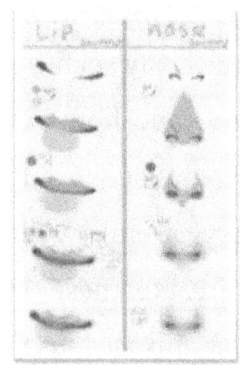

*Image: Creative commons attribution: saviroosje*

specific detail on the areas of the face and how to capture them in watercolor. I tend to lightly draw everything and then pick it up and color and shade it.

## Use of a grid

As for other images that you draw, using a grid and your iPad is a wonderful way to get all the details in the right places. If you look at the image below, you will see why this is.

The artist on DeviantArt.com with the name of Wicked used a grid to produce an image and you can see that you can count the squares and make sure that the mouth, eyes and nose are all

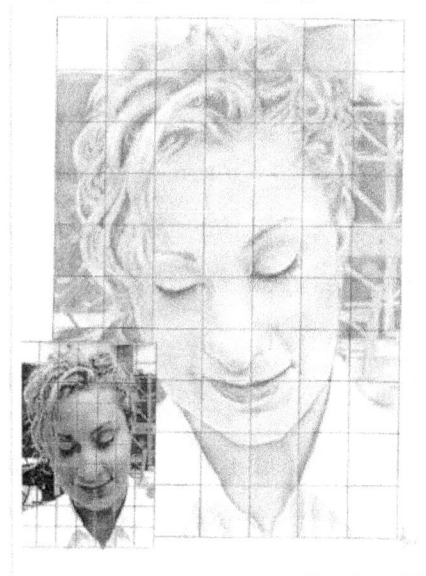

correctly placed in the correct square. When I did portraits using this manner of transposition, I found that I got much sharper images because I wasn't so afraid of where to place all of the features. Starting from one square at the bottom, start to draw in the detail and you build up an image which is not only accurate but which can be worked on until the image is an exact likeness of the subject with the addition of skin tones and water color. This is a great method for using when you want to get an accurate picture from a photograph as well and if you have a decent size of photo you can actually draw the grid onto the photograph and then do the same thing on your paper, transposing the image square by square onto your paper. This helps you to get things accurate but you will be tempted to change things when you stand at a distance and see discrepancies. This is common and nothing to worry about. It takes a wonderful artist to get it all right first time. At least all of the features of the face, the shape of the head, the hairline and the neck will be all in the right place. The rest is something that you have time to work on when you start to paint.

## Eyes

The images shown above show eyes from different angles. When you start to paint portraits, you will have to be very aware of the anatomical features of the eye and that takes a lot of observation. The line just above the eyelids at the bottom of the eye is one that gives eyes great detail. Look how the lashes reflect in the first image and how a spot of white has been used in both of the photographs above to give the eye its sense of reflection.

Again, as in much watercolor work, you work from the back color upward. The idea is that you layer your work, so that the features you want to see in your picture are gradually built up to provide the finished image of the eyes. It is worth noting that the placement of the eyes can totally change the image. Thus, if you find that your pencil sketch places them too close together or far apart, it's worthwhile correcting that before going further with the image, since the actual fine detail will make them look ever more out of proportion.

The placement of the eyebrows and the correct distance from the eye and nose is also vital to accuracy. These are areas which take a lot of concentration and are 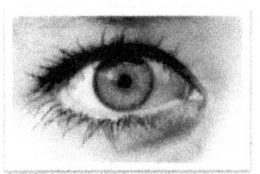 also areas which can be really helped by using the grid method of drawing, since their 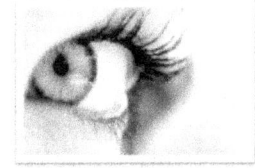 placement will be much more accurate than if simply drawn from what you see.

## Hair

Although you may think of hair as being a set color, that's actually far from the truth. There are so many reflective colors in hair. You will find that you can make this look very detailed in watercolor painting and that your shadows are every bit as important as the colors that are reflected on the surface of the hair, and which are picked out with your detail paintbrush.

If you want to find help with this or tips about where you are going wrong, DeviantArt.com is a great website to find examples of hair and how it has been painted. The above example from an artist named Denitsed is a great example, because you see all the reflections in the 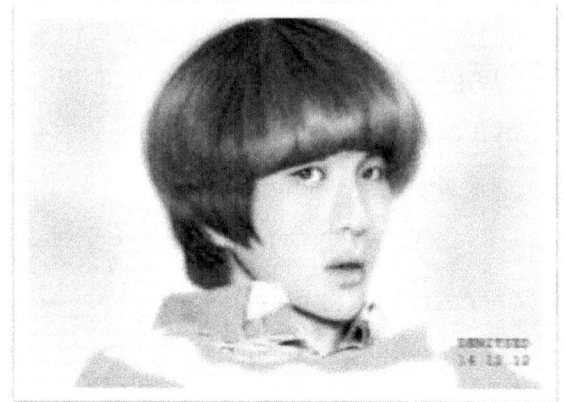 color of the hair and it looks realistic enough as well as looking shiny and healthy. It takes a lot of practice to get hair that accurately painted, but that's not the only kind of painting used for hair. Think of hair as flowing. Often this is painted using wet on wet but filling the fine detail in after the actual shades have blended together using this method.

During the wet on wet part of painting the hair, you can blend all the different colors that you see to give depth, shadow and color and then the reflections are added with lighter colors and very fine brushwork.

Look at examples in Google Images because you may just find the style that you like the best and can use this as an example. It is too tempting to think of hair as either being blonde, brunette or black but when you are painting a portrait, use the colors that you see rather than using your preconception of what you see. Often you will see much more if you can take the photo with an iPad and then blow up the area of the hair, giving you all the detail in the color that is true to the image. That's one of the benefits of using the iPad. You simply stretch the image to look in detail at the area that you want to paint.

All of these tips will help you in your drawing of the face and the background, which you use, can be pretty abstract and either in a darker shade, which shows off the facial features well or can be a mixture of pastel shades that are muted, so that the face is always the most important part of the picture.

# CHAPTER TEN

# Still Life Painting

Classic painting of still life is good practice for the watercolor painter. Not only do you have a limited amount of information to place on your paper, but also you don't have to contend with models that may move, or scenery that changes so much because of the climatic conditions. With still life painting, you do have changes of light which may affect how you picture your given subject. If you 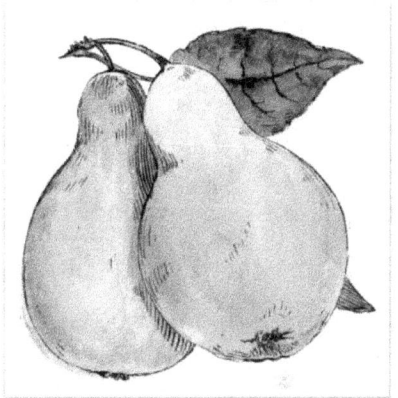 have a place where you can sit comfortably and observe your still life subject in reasonable light, this helps.

A great example of a subject for your first water color still life would be fruit. Because its skin is not difficult to paint and consists merely of tones, it's much easier than trying to reproduce elements such as glass, which take a more experienced painter. Look at these pears and you will see that the basic outline is fairly straightforward and that the image is impressive, even though the subject matter used is simple.

Although you may think this is too simple, look at the way that the shades have been mixed because there is skill in getting the skins of the fruit in accurate colors. A basic all over wash of the lightest color would then be added to, in order to produce shadow and shape. The pears look three dimensional because of the color and shading. The leaf and stem may simply look dark green, but look closely because the number of shades used may amaze you. When you are using a palette, you can mix various depths of the same color all on the same palette and use it randomly so that the color you are using corresponds with that displayed on the fruit you are painting.

Try to place your still life objects in an artistically composed way so that the end product is pleasing to the eye. Fruit and flowers are great objects to begin your watercolor painting experience because you can do them in the privacy of your home and learn how to mix your colors on your palette to get the best results. Remember, for a wash, the paint is mixed with a larger quantity of water, though the more detail or more color you wish to produce, the less water is used. Only work on an area that has been washed, if you want the colors to run together. If not, wait until the wash is dried and then work on top of the base color to build up your detail.

## Using traced images

In the initial stages of working with watercolors, why not use some stock images to get your shapes and proportions? These will help you to learn composition and you can find many on the Internet, by Googling the words "Drawing fruit" or "drawing flowers" and print them. Once printed you can use tracing paper to transfer the image onto your paper, though it's best to do this with pencil. When you have traced the image, turn the tracing paper over and lightly rub against the lines you drew with pencil so that these show up on your paper. These can be used as your sketch and the color and practice of painting detail can be your introduction to producing great quality pictures.

The picture below is typical of a stock picture and there are great books available from Dover Publications, which have many stock items in the style that you wish to paint. These are always useful for those times when you just want to get started and are uninspired or don't have enough confidence in your own ability.

A somewhat bland camellia picture can be turned into a masterpiece with clever use of background paint and then very subtle color for the petals, and perhaps darker colors for the leaves.

Give it a try and see if you can find stock images that you can paint for greetings cards and small projects. Watercolors are very versatile and although people think of them as creating pictures with soft coloring, the depth of the coloring is really your individual choice. It is the overall presentation that is more important than the depth of color. By experimenting with dilution, you begin to understand your paints better and which brushes can be used to give your painting more detail.

As you get more advanced, you will find that you will want to invest in finer brushes to help you with your detailing and that's quite normal. Some floral artists actually use brushes with one bristle because the detail that they use is so fine. Watercolor artists who paint miniatures are particularly prone to using this measure of detail because being miniature, the picture needs that definition more than on a full sized image, to take the viewer's eye into the complexity of the painting.

# CHAPTER ELEVEN

# Taking Your Painting Out on Location

There are several reasons for mentioning this. As a new painter in water color, the chances are that you haven't thought about what a good medium this is to go out and enjoy. Once you get over your initial nervousness, actually taking your work outdoors can be very enjoyable indeed.

If you are going to do this, don't take the whole kit. You don't need it. You need your pencil and sharpener to sketch the initial sketch, but as far as colors goes, a good quality paint box is the best bet which uses block water color. I have one that I keep for this purpose. I invested in an easel but it's one of the folding kind that is less obtrusive and easier to carry. The trouble is that if you go full out with a full sized easel, people who walk by you will be expecting great things when they look over your shoulder. If you are a little nervous about that happening, you can even use a hard backed water color drawing pad, which gives you the option of shading your work when you don't want people to stare at it. The problem is that people are curious and although I used to find it pretty irritating, actually got to relax after a while and found that these are just people who are curious and some turned out to be good friends and people who asked for commissions. Take the minimum of brushes. You don't need them all, but do make sure that you have a water container of some sort and a roll of kitchen paper. I use a baby food bottle. It's small and compact and has a screw lid, so I can ditch the water and then place it easily into my bag to go home.

You can get bags for artists, but I think that if you put your own together you get a better feel for all of the things that you need and can personalize it more by having a space for your drinks and food as well as your art supplies. Places which are good for practicing watercolor are:

- Country scenes out in the open
- Seaside locations
- Places of architectural interest
- Places which offer flowers and natural growth
- Riverside locations

These are the ideals but look for something else as well. You need to have agreeable colors and some scenery really does give you this naturally while other places look pretty bland. Remember the composition is everything so you will need to find a place where you can be seated for a long period of time without getting in anyone's way. I have one of those folding stools which is very light and have a slot for it on the side of my bag.

## The changing of the light

Sometimes you look at a scene and think it's perfect. Then a dark cloud comes over and you have lost the image forever. The trouble with a natural environment is that it is for ever changing and you can expect even the shadow to change places during the course of a day. Thus, if you have an iPad you can capture photographs from the stance that you have chosen at different times of the day and when you get back home can work on the picture even more so that the best view is used when the shadow was perfect. You can do the same with a digital camera and put the image onto your computer screen to give you a good clear image to work from. It's not copying. It is actually grabbing a moment in time when the light was perfect and capturing it ready for your painting.

## Weather

Obviously the best weather for water color painting is going to be dry weather, but I have found that some winter scenes are wonderful. Just make sure that you take lots of hot drink with you and buy yourself a pair of fingerless gloves! These will help to protect your hands. The color in winter is sometimes more suited to watercolor because of the lighting although other seasons are great for other reasons. For example, the bright sparkling colors of autumn are very good indeed, but be sure to peg your paper to the easel if you use one because the winds can pick up pretty fast.

## Getting together a group

It's a great idea to join an art class because you will be taken into the outdoor environment in a group and that makes you feel less vulnerable. If you do join a class, a teacher is likely to encourage you to take much more than you usually need to take when you go alone. They tend to be a little stuffy about teaching you the use of different brushes and it's their work to do that, but when you step from being in a class to being out there on your own or with friends, you don't need all of those brushes. You really don't. Go along with it for the classes because you will pick up some very good tips on how to use special brushes for specific purposes. I learned a great trick with a stippling brush used to create the leaves on a distant tree which were later tidied up with a detailing brush. It took a lot of detailed and time consuming work out of the task at hand and it's a trick that I have used ever since.

## How to deal with people who are nosy

Over the course of the last 15 years, I have found that I have met a variety of people while I am out painting. Some will look and make an "umm" noise and walk away. Others will ask questions and may even ask if they can be in the picture. I had a child that made a wonderful model for one country scene and he was just out riding his bike and bored. Getting him to sit still long enough wasn't going to be an easy task, but what I did was do an outline, then take a photo with the iPad and ask him for his address. His parents were delighted with the results and insisted on paying me for the picture, even though I was quite happy to give it to them.

You may find that you get the pet brigade when you are out there and they can be a little bit annoying. They want to commission you to draw their pooch or their cat and tend to be the kind of people who stick around for hours. The thing is that art attracts people. You may get advice from well-meaning people. You may get criticism but that's pretty unlikely. I think that people who have negative things to say tend to walk past quietly and think them rather than saying them.

The whole point is that you have chosen a public place and have to take it all very lightly. Let them know you're a beginner if that gives you a little more confidence and perhaps they will be gentle with you. I tended to ignore it but got very uptight about it at first. When I started to relax I found that all of those fears went into the background and you simple enjoy the experience because that's what it's really all about.

# CHAPTER TWELVE

# Looking After Your Tools

**W**hen you have finished your painting for the day, you need to get into a routine of washing your paintbrushes thoroughly. You can run these under a warm tap but make sure that all paint is removed from the stock of the brush, which is the area where the bristles are fastened to the handle. This area is prone to get clogged with paint. Be gentle when you are cleaning the brushes and always respect the flow of the bristles, never pulling them to the sides to get the brush clean. As they are water soluble, you should find this fairly straightforward.

You can dry off the brushes with a piece of kitchen paper, though make sure that the bristles are straight when you place them into a storage container, bristles upward, so that they are ready for the next use.

Your palette will need cleaning and this can usually be cleaned adequately under a running tap. Some stubborn areas may need to soak for a short while and some staining may occur to your palette but this won't impede your future work.

Allow your paintings space to dry and never stack them before they are sufficiently dry to do so. If you are working in a watercolor artist's booklet, then keep the page open until all of the paint is dry to avoid smudging.

If you are using block paints, you can remove any excess liquid with a sponge and then wipe the paint pots so that your paints are relatively clean. It isn't necessary to have them spotless and many artists leave their paint boxes to air dry. Even if some colors are a little messy, it won't impede your progress the next time that you start to paint. Throw away your water and keep your jar for water separate so that it's ready for next time.

# Conclusion

**N**ow that you have made the move and bought this book as your introduction to basic watercolor painting, you have also begun your journey into the land of discovery. Every artist will find techniques that surprise and delight them. This is all part of the process. For example, try running colors into each other intentionally as some of the affects you can create can be stunningly beautiful and resemble, to a certain degree, the colors of nature. Practice painting fine detail until your hands are able to work with confidence. There is so much for you to learn, though now you have the paints, the brushes and the palette, be sure to take this out regularly and watch your own skills develop.

While many leave their artistic endeavors until late in their lifetimes, this is an easy art to incorporate into your life. The paints don't take up a great deal of space and because of the easy application of water colors, these are paints which can be taken out and used spontaneously when you find you have time on your hands. Each time you do, you will find that your techniques improve and that you can produce reasonable pictures to hang on the walls, or use the craft for greetings cards for friends or small portraits.

If you have children, perhaps you can even encourage them to try out their artistic skills with this medium which is easy to use and which is easy to clean up after them. Try your hand at using vignettes, which are cardboard edges that sit on your paper while you work. When you take away the vignette, you are left with a delightful edging to your work. These are super for images of people but also very good for images of flowers and landscapes. Add a little three-dimensional effect after the vignette has been taken away, by extending floral stems or branches into the white area at the end of the image.

Watercolor painting is a joy and now that you have started, be sure to try different textures and color combinations, as you will see how quickly a change of coloring on a similar design can transform the picture entirely.

You are recommended to buy good quality materials for your watercolor work. These are not expensive, but are worth investing in because they give so much better results. Brushes made from bristles will wear and last better than their synthetic counterparts, and good quality watercolors will have pigments, which give bright colors and more accurate finishes once the paint has dried. Good quality artist's paper for your water colors is an essential since inferior paper will encourage bleeding of colors and even warping of the paper during the painting process, thus giving disappointing results.

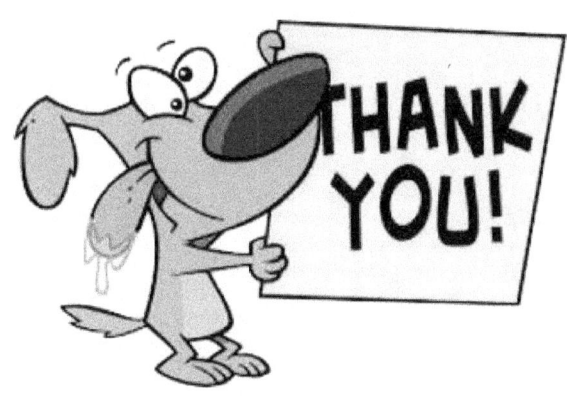

# FREE BONUS GUIDE

# Fundamentals of Successful Thinking

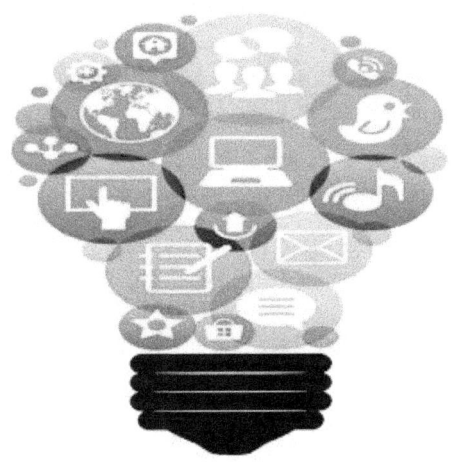

Free **Bonus "Instant Access"** Click Below For Your Bonus:

https://success321.leadpages.co/fundamentals-of-successful-thinking/

# Checkout My Other Books

- http://www.amazon.com/Painting-Box-Acrylic-Guide-Beginners-ebook/dp/B00UTNRGNW/ref=sr_1_3?s=digital-text&ie=UTF8&qid=1430259945&sr=1-3&keywords=painting

- http://www.amazon.com/Acrylic-Painting-Techniques-Landscape-Everything-ebook/dp/B00Q3SRQJG/ref=sr_1_7?s=digital-text&ie=UTF8&qid=1430259945&sr=1-7&keywords=painting

- http://www.amazon.com/Oil-Painting-Complete-Beginners-Techniques-ebook/dp/B00S1XXIZM/ref=sr_1_4?s=digital-text&ie=UTF8&qid=1430260043&sr=1-4&keywords=oil+painting

•